Children's
Step by step
fun-to-cook book

Alison Holst

Illustrated by Seth Kelly

This book is dedicated to the thousands of young people who told Dame Alison Holst what they would like to cook. The recipes have all been test-cooked by a twelve-year-old.

Before You Start

Before you make any recipe from this book, you need to read it right through, find all the ingredients you need, measure them carefully, then combine them exactly in the way the recipe tells you!

If you are careful, you should get the same good results every time you make a particular recipe.

All the cup and spoon measures in this book are levelled off, not heaped up or pushed down hard, unless the recipe tells you differently. Always double check that you are using the correct measure. You will find it easier and quicker if you use sets of metric measuring cups and spoons. Use a set of spoons where a tablespoon holds 15mls, a teaspoon 5mls, and there are half and quarter teaspoon measures to use for very small amounts.

It is much easier measuring with a set of measuring cups rather than part-filling a 1 cup measure. You need a half-cup measure and a quarter-cup measure as well. In the pictures, a 1 cup measure is red, a 3/4 cup measure is orange, a 1/2 cup measure is yellow and a 1/4 cup measure is green.

Stir the flour, then spoon it into the cup. Don't shake or bang the cup.

Measure flour, sugar, chocolate chips & salt into a bowl. Mix with a fork.

In steps where a sharp knife is used the word SHARP is written in blue, to remind you to take care or get help.

SHARP!

Slice the mushrooms. Chop up the tomato (and throw away the seeds).

SHARP!

Slice the spring onion. Use the white part and about half the green leaves.

Where food is fried in very hot oil, and great care is needed, the word HOT is written in the corner.

Where food is heated to a lower temperature, there is no word in the corner, but the picture frame has a red glow around it. Again, take care, or ask for help.

Bake for 12 minutes or until it looks golden brown underneath.

HOT!

Check oil is hot by dropping in some batter. It should brown in a minute.

If you are using an electric appliance, always follow the manufacturer's instructions.

You will see special stirrers used in some of the pictures. These are easy to use and do a very good job. See the back page for details about buying them.

I hope that you have fun cooking these recipes, and also eating the food you have prepared!

Contents

Nachos

Find everything you need before you start cooking

Spicy Beans:
1 medium-sized onion
2 tsp olive or Canola oil
1 large clove garlic
1 tsp ground cumin
1/2 tsp oregano
about 1/4 tsp chilli powder
425g can baked beans
2 Tbsp tomato paste

250g packet of corn chips
about 1 cup grated tasty
  cheese
about 1/2 cup low-fat
  sour cream

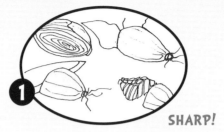

SHARP!

Cut onion in half, top to bottom, skin, then chop onion finely. Put in pan.

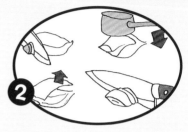

Cook in oil, medium heat. Cut root off garlic, then squash, peel & chop.

Stir garlic, cumin, oregano and chilli powder into pan with onion.

Stir in baked beans & tomato paste, cook for 5 minutes, then turn off.

Spread chips on grill tray. Sprinkle with cheese and grill until it melts.

OR Microwave corn chips and cheese in batches until the cheese melts.

7

Cook all the chips and cheese.
Pile hot cheesy chips on a plate.

8

Serve with bowls of warm spicy
beans and sour cream for dipping.

For a change:

Pile spicy bean dip in centre of
platter, arrange chips around it,
sprinkle with cheese and grill.

Add wedges of tomato and avocado
or guacamole if you like.

Who can resist corn chips topped with
grilled cheese, and served with a spicy
bean mixture and sour cream so you can
spoon on the amounts you want!

Find everything you need before you start cooking

For 2 people:
2 large potatoes, 250g each
2 Tbsp flour
1 Tbsp grated parmesan cheese
1/2 tsp curry powder
1/2 tsp paprika
1/2 tsp ground cumin
1/4 tsp garlic or onion salt or 1/8 tsp plain salt
2 Tbsp olive or other oil
sour cream for dipping

Put oven tray below the middle. Turn oven on to heat at 250°C.

SHARP!

Scrub potatoes, cut lengthwise into half, then quarters, then eighths.

As you cut up the potatoes, put them into a large bowl of cold water.

Put everything else, except oil and cream, into a LARGE dry plastic bag.

Spread 1 Tbsp oil over a large shallow metal baking tin.

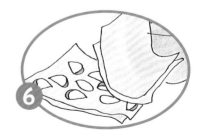

Drain potatoes and dry well with paper towels. Put back in dried bowl.

7

Pour remaining 1 Tbsp oil over them and turn them to coat completely.

8

Put in bag with flour, etc. Close bag so it holds air too. Shake well.

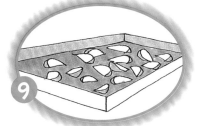

9

Lie wedges flat in tin. Bake 20–30 minutes, until tender & golden brown.

Wedges seem to be everybody's favourite potato recipe. They disappear so fast you need to make lots more than you think you need!

Toasted Cheese Sandwiches

It is hard to believe how good something as easy as this can be! It's great for a quick weekend snack or an after-school pick-me-up!

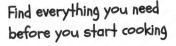

Find everything you need before you start cooking

2 slices of toast bread
butter
slices of cheese
optional extras
   (see later)

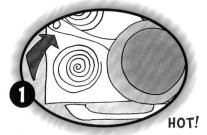

HOT!

Put a large non-stick frypan on stove (handle to back) on low heat.

Warm butter so it will spread smoothly or use semi-soft butter.

Butter both bread slices evenly but not too thickly, right to the edges.

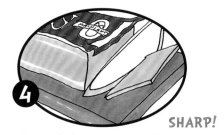

SHARP!

Cut slices of cheese to cover the unbuttered side of one slice.

Spread unbuttered side of the other slice with chutney, etc. if you like.

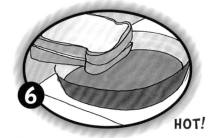

HOT!

Make sandwich with buttered sides out and carefully place on hot pan.

HOT!

Cook until bottom is golden brown, then turn over. Cook the other side.

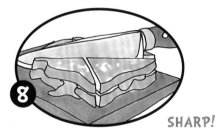

SHARP!

Lift on to a board and cut in strips or triangles with a sharp knife.

Eat while warm, either by itself or with soup, a salad or fresh fruit.

Other fillings you can put in with the cheese if you like are:

slices of tomato

slices of raw apple

slices of banana

thinly sliced ham

cucumber or other pickles

These cheeses make great toasted sandwiches:

Colby (smooth and creamy)

Mild (young cheddar)

Tasty (mature cheddar)

Edam (reduced fat)

Vintage (full of flavour)

Gruyere (Swiss)

Raclette (deliciously different)

Hawaiian Pizza

Find everything you need before you start cooking

For 2 people:
1/2 cup milk
1 Tbsp olive or other oil
1 cup self-raising flour
1 Tbsp tomato paste
1 Tbsp water
1/4 tsp crumbled dried
    oregano

Toppings:
1/2 cup chopped ham
    or luncheon sausage
    or 1/4 cup chopped
    salami
1/2 cup chopped canned
    pineapple
1 cup grated cheese
1/4 cup chopped tomato

Put the oven rack just below middle. Turn the oven on to heat at 220°C.

Put the milk and oil in a medium-sized bowl and mix well with a fork.

Add the flour and mix with the fork, then your hand, to form a ball.

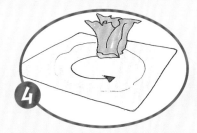

So pizza doesn't stick, rub butter in a 30cm circle on a baking tray.

Roll out dough on this, until it is 30cm round. Fold in edges all round.

Mix tomato paste, water and crumbled oregano and spread evenly on pizza.

Cover with ham and pineapple, then sprinkle cheese and tomato on top.

Bake for 12 minutes or until it looks golden brown underneath.

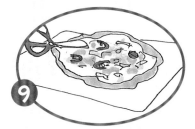

Cut in wedges with kitchen scissors and eat before it gets cold.

After you have made this a couple of times, you'll be able to make pizza really fast and easily. Try different toppings for a change, too.

Crispy Pork Wontons

These are fun to make and delicious to eat. Be very careful if you fry them, or take the easy way and bake them — they are almost as good!

Find everything you need before you start cooking

40–50 wonton skins

400g pork mince
1 Tbsp lemon juice
2 Tbsp soy sauce
1 Tbsp cornflour
1 tsp (Asian) sesame oil
2–3 spring onions

Canola oil or other oil
dipping sauce
tongs

1 Thaw wonton skins if necessary. Keep them wrapped. Don't let them dry out.

2 Put the minced pork in a bowl. Mix in the next four things, using a fork.

SHARP!

3 Chop spring onions into thin slices, and add them too. Mix well.

4 Divide filling in four parts, then each part in 10 small blobs.

HOT!

5 Heat oil 1 cm deep in a small pot or turn oven on to heat at 225°C.

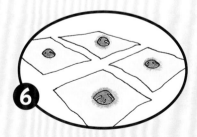

6 Take 4 wonton skins at a time. Put one blob on the middle of each.

7 Dampen one side with a little water, fold edge over. Press sides together.

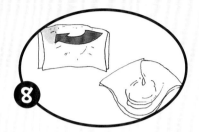

8 Leave flat for easier frying, or fold over, dampening parts which touch.

9 Lower carefully into hot oil. Adjust heat so wontons brown in 1 minute.

HOT!

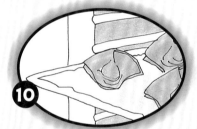

10 OR brush both sides with oil. Bake on baking paper at for 225°C 10 minutes.

11 Drain cooked wontons on paper towels. Eat hot with sauce for dipping.

Cheesy Potatoes or Pizza Potatoes

Find everything you need before you start cooking

1 large potato
   (200–300g)
1 tsp milk
1/4–1/2 cup grated tasty
   cheese

For Pizza Potatoes add:
1 slice salami, chopped
   fine
1/4 tomato without
   seeds, chopped
1/2 spring onion, chopped

2 tsp extra grated cheese

1 SHARP!

Scrub, then dry the potato, then pierce it deeply 4 times with a pointed knife.

2 Bake it in the middle of the microwave, turning it over after half the time.

3 A 200g potato should cook in 5 minutes and a 300g potato in 7 minutes.

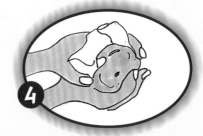

4 Leave it for 3 minutes, then hold in a cloth and squeeze gently all over.

5 Halve the potato. Using a teaspoon, scoop the inside part into a bowl.

6 Add the milk and grated cheese to taste. Mix with fork until smooth and creamy.

Stir in the other flavourings if you like. Pile filling back into skins.

Microwave 30 seconds to reheat, then sprinkle with a little extra cheese.

Brown under a hot grill for about a minute or eat without browning top.

You can make a quick snack that is very tasty and filling if you have a microwave oven, a potato and some cheese! Extra flavourings are good too.

Mini Hot Dogs

Nearly everyone is surprised to find just how good these taste. They make a few saveloys go a long way, and they are remarkably filling, too.

Find everything you need before you start cooking

For 4 people:

4 saveloys
1 large egg
1/2 cup milk
1 cup self-raising flour
1/2 tsp curry powder
1/2 tsp paprika
1/2 tsp salt

wooden iceblock sticks
oil for frying
tongs

HOT!

Heat oil 7mm deep in a frypan (200°C). Turn pan handle to back of stove.

SHARP!

While oil heats slowly, run a sharp knife along saveloys. Peel off skin.

SHARP!

Slice each saveloy diagonally in 5 or 6 slices using a serrated knife.

Push iceblock sticks in, so they look like suckers, and will lie flat.

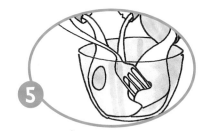

Put the egg and milk in a bowl and beat with a fork until evenly mixed.

Sift flour, curry, paprika and salt into bowl. Stir in but don't overmix.

7 **HOT!**

Check oil is hot by dropping in some batter. It should brown in a minute.

8

Tilt the bowl and turn the hot dog in batter so all the saveloy is covered.

9 **HOT!**

Using tongs, carefully place hot dogs in pan. TAKE CARE NOT TO SPLASH.

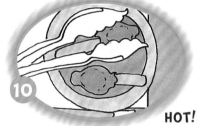

10 **HOT!**

When bottom is golden turn over, using tongs to hold each side.

11

When golden, lift onto paper towel. Serve hot, dipped in tomato sauce.

Crustless Corn Quiche

Find everything you need before you start cooking

For 4–6 people:

3 large or 4 smaller eggs
1 cup milk
1/2 cup self-raising flour
1/2 tsp salt
425g can creamed corn
1 1/2 cups grated tasty
  cheese

If you like,
add one or all these:
1–2 cups chopped, cooked
  potatoes
2 spring onions, chopped
2 rashers bacon, cooked
  and chopped

1 or 2 sliced tomatoes to
go on top, if you like.

1 Put the oven rack just below the middle. Turn the oven on to 220°C.

2 Find a 20cm square tin (or a 23cm square tin if you add the potatoes).

3 Put eggs, milk, flour and salt in a large bowl. Beat until smooth.

4 Stir in corn, 1 cup cheese, and any or all of the next three suggestions.

5 Butter or spray the baking tin or dish. Pour the mixture into it.

6 If using them, put tomatoes on top. Sprinkle with the rest of the cheese.

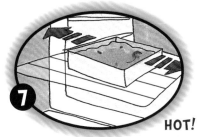

HOT!

Bake for 20–30 minutes or until the centre doesn't wobble when jiggled.

SHARP!

Take out and leave to stand for 10–15 minutes before cutting in pieces.

Lift carefully from the tin. Quiche is good with a salad and bread rolls.

This quiche doesn't have a pastry shell, but forms a light crust as it cooks. It's good hot or warm, and leftovers go well in packed lunches.

Corn Fritters

Always keep a can of corn in your cupboard, since corn fritters are so popular, and so useful for quick meals and snacks.

Find everything you need before you start cooking

For 4–6 people:

425g can whole kernel corn
1 large egg
1 cup self-raising flour

oil for frying
tongs for turning

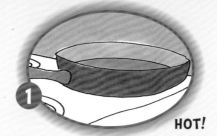

HOT!

Heat oil 7mm deep in a frypan (200°C). Turn pan handle to back of stove.

Open can of corn. Fill a 1/4 cup measure with some of the liquid.

Drain the rest of the liquid into a glass – you probably won't need it.

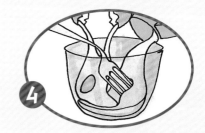

With a fork, mix measured corn liquid and egg together in a large bowl.

Add drained corn and flour. Stir together but don't mix too much.

If mixture is too thick add more liquid. If too runny, add more flour.

7 Using two spoons, very carefully place small blobs in the hot oil.

HOT!

8 When bottom of each is golden-brown turn over carefully, using tongs.

HOT!

9 When both sides are golden brown lift onto crumpled paper towels to drain.

10 Eat while hot. Dip in tomato sauce or pour maple or golden syrup over them.

For a change:

You can make corn cakes instead of fritters from this recipe if you like. Add 1 tablespoon of melted butter with the egg. Thin mixture with a little extra milk so it spreads like pikelets.

Cook spoonfuls of the mixture like pikelets on page 42.

Find everything you need before you start cooking

For 1–2 people:

about 4 button
   mushrooms
1 large tomato
1 spring onion
2 large eggs
1/4 cup milk
1/4 tsp salt
1 Tbsp butter
1/4 cup grated tasty
   cheese
1 or 2 slices freshly made
   toast

SHARP!

Slice the mushrooms. Chop up the tomato (and throw away the seeds).

SHARP!

Slice the spring onion. Use the white part and about half the green leaves.

Break the eggs into a bowl, add the milk and salt and beat with a fork.

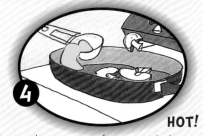

HOT!

Put mushrooms in a frypan with the butter. Heat until lightly browned.

Stir in the tomato and spring onion. When warm, pour in the egg mixture.

When egg starts to set, push a fish slice across the bottom of the pan.

7

Let all the top, uncooked part run underneath. Sprinkle on the cheese.

8

While the top still looks shiny, pile the scramble carefully on the toast.

For a change:

Instead of cooking mushrooms and tomatoes, sizzle some chopped up, cooked potatoes in the pan before adding the egg and the cheese.

When you add some mushrooms, tomatoes and cheese to scrambled eggs, and put the lot on toast, you finish up with a quick, easy and tasty meal!

Hamburgers

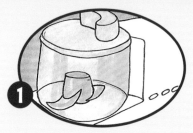

If you have a food processor, mix all the pattie ingredients in it.

OR break bread into small pieces and stir with the milk in a large bowl.

SHARP!

Slice the spring onions very finely or peel the onion, then grate half of it.

Mix spring onion or grated onion and the sauces through the soft bread.

Add the meat, broken in 10–12 blobs. Stir until everything is well mixed.

With wet hands, make 6 equal pieces. Shape patties as wide as the buns.

Prepare the cheese, tomato, lettuce, sauce, and mustard to go in the buns.

HOT!

Split buns and butter lightly. Brown cut sides in hot pan or under grill.

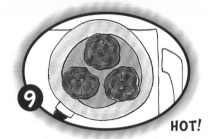

HOT!

Heat a large frypan. When hot, drip in a little oil and add 2 or 3 patties.

HOT!

Cook patties on high heat until brown on both sides. Turn after 2 minutes.

These hamburgers are big and juicy. They don't take long to make or cost much. Put whatever you like best in the bun with the pattie.

Put burgers in the warm buns with your favourite toppings. Enjoy!

Cheesy Pieburgers

Everybody loves these! Use lower fat pastry for them if you can. Put extras in the freezer for a quick meal, a picnic, or packed lunches.

Find everything you need before you start cooking

1 egg
500g minced beef
1/4 cup tomato sauce
2 Tbsp flour
1 packet onion soup

2 sheets pre-rolled pastry (150 g each)
1/2 cup grated tasty cheese
parmesan cheese if you like

Put the oven rack below the middle. Turn the oven on to heat at 200°C.

Break egg in a large bowl and beat to mix. Pour half into a cup & put aside.

Put mince, sauce, flour and soup mix in bowl with 1/2 egg. Mix everything.

Roll the pastry thinly on a floured bench to make two 30–35cm squares.

Divide the meat into nine equal blobs. Put these on one sheet of the pastry.

Put the cheese on top of the meat. Brush water on pastry between meat.

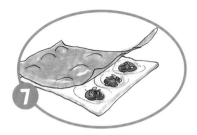

Put the other pastry on top. Press it down on bottom pastry around meat.

SHARP!

Cut between the meat into squares. Trim edges. Make a cut on each pie.

Brush reserved egg all over pastry. Decorate with trimmings if you like.

Sprinkle with parmesan cheese and lift carefully onto a baking tray.

HOT!

Bake 30 minutes, until golden brown, then cool on rack. Best eaten warm.

Spanish Potato Omelet

Even though it doesn't sound very interesting, this is a delicious omelet, easily made for a meal or snack at any time of day. Try it!

Find everything you need before you start cooking

3 fairly big potatoes
3 Tbsp olive or Canola oil
2 large eggs
1/2 tsp salt

For a change:

Cook a chopped onion with the potato, or add chopped fresh herbs to the egg mixture.

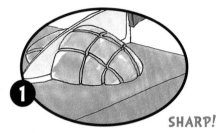

SHARP!

1 Scrub the potatoes. Cut them in 1cm slices, then 1cm cubes, on a board.

HOT!

2 Put the oil in a small non-stick frypan and warm on medium heat.

3 Slide the potato cubes into the pan and put a lid on straight away.

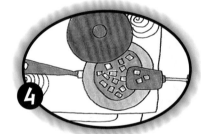

4 Cook for 7–8 minutes, stirring at times, until potatoes are tender.

5 In a large bowl beat eggs and salt with a fork, just until combined.

6 Lift the cooked potatoes into bowl with egg, leaving any oil in the pan.

Stir well, then tip back into hot pan.
Cover, cook until nearly set, 3 min.

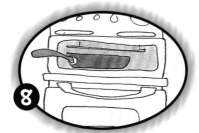

Brown and set the top under a hot grill.
Don't let pan handle burn though!

OR slide omelet onto plate, then flip
back into pan and brown the top.

Macaroni Cheese

Everybody's favourite. It is good plain, but you can make interesting variations when you feel like a change.

Find everything you need before you start cooking

for 2-4 people:

2 cups macaroni
25g (2 Tbsp) butter
2 Tbsp flour
1 1/2 cups milk
2 cups grated tasty
  cheese
1/4-1/2 tsp salt, optional

Optional topping:
1 Tbsp butter
2 slices bread

1 HOT!

Put 8 cups of water and 1 1/2 tsp salt in a pot and heat until the water boils.

2

Stir in macaroni, then boil uncovered until tender, about 10 minutes.

3

In another pot, melt the butter, then stir in the flour until it is smooth.

4

Pour in half the milk and heat until it is thick, stirring all the time.

5

Add the rest of the milk and heat and stir until sauce is thick and smooth.

6

Turn off heat, then add grated cheese and stir until silky smooth.

Drain the cooked macaroni and stir it into the sauce. Add salt to taste.

Eat as is, or put into a baking dish and sprinkle with buttered crumbs.

Bake at 190°C until the crumbs are golden brown and the edges bubble.

To make buttered crumbs:

Melt 1 Tbsp butter in a frypan or microwave dish. Grate, crumble, or chop 2 slices of bread in a food processor. Mix crumbs with the melted butter.

For a change, stir into the sauce, with the macaroni:

1 - 2 cups of cooked broccoli
1 cup drained whole kernel corn
1/2 cup drained crushed pineapple
about 1/2 cup chopped ham
If you add corn or pineapple, replace 1/2 cup milk with 1/2 cup can liquid.

French Toast

Fancy being able to make something so good from leftover bread! It's a great breakfast and an easy snack at other times when hunger pangs strike!

Find everything you need before you start cooking

1 large egg
1 Tbsp milk
1 tsp sugar, if you like
2 slices bread
2 tsp butter for cooking
(in 1/2 teaspoon pieces)

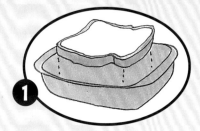

1 Find a shallow bowl big enough to hold a slice of bread, lying flat.

2 Break in the egg, add milk and sugar and beat with a fork or stirrer.

3 Dip bread in mixture so each side is coated, then lie slices in a flat dish.

4 Pour any leftover egg mixture on the bread, so it can soak it up.

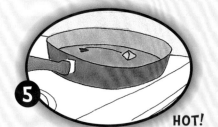

HOT!

5 Warm pan on medium heat, drop in 1/2 teaspoon butter and swirl it round.

HOT!

6 When butter bubbles, before it browns, put in one slice of the bread.

Turn when golden brown, after about a minute, and add a little more butter.

If you like, grill some bacon and slice a banana while French Toast cooks.

Cut slices in half if you like. Serve warm with maple or golden syrup.

Oaty Pancakes

Dot a little butter on each pancake, pile them up, pour syrup over the lot, add some sliced banana, and you have a breakfast everyone loves!

Find everything you need before you start cooking

3/4 cup milk
3/4 cup rolled oats
1 large egg
1/2 cup self-raising flour
3 Tbsp sugar
1/2 tsp salt
25g (2 Tbsp) butter

Pour the milk over the oats and leave to stand for a few minutes.

Add egg and beat with a fork. Sift in flour, sugar and salt (DON'T MIX).

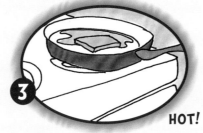

HOT!

Melt the butter in a non-stick pan in which pancakes will cook later.

Add melted butter to bowl and mix everything. (DON'T MIX TOO MUCH.)

Pour some pancake mixture into the hot pan to make a round pancake.

When bubbles burst on top of the pancake, turn it over.

Cook second side until the centre springs back when lightly pressed.

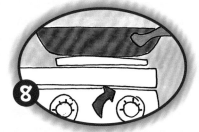

Adjust the heat if necessary, so next pancakes are golden brown.

Serve warm, singly or stacked, with butter and syrup or jam.

Fruity Smoothies

Find everything you need before you start cooking

For 3-4 large smoothies:

1 small banana and/or
   4 ripe strawberries
1/2 cup orange juice
1/2 cup fat-free milk
about 1 tsp maple syrup
or sugar
1/4 tsp vanilla, if you like

1 Mash the peeled banana and/or the strawberries, using a fork.

2 Put the mashed fruit in a food processor.

3 Add the orange juice and turn on the machine. Process until smooth.

4 Pour in the cold milk and keep processing until very thick.

5 Add maple syrup or sugar to taste, and vanilla if you like.

6 Pour into glasses. Serve with thick straws and teaspoons. Enjoy!

Milky Ice Blocks

Just the thing to cool you down on hot days. Keep a supply in the freezer all summer!

Find everything you need before you start cooking

1 cup orange juice
1 cup milk
1 Tbsp sugar

Measure the orange juice and milk into a jug.

Add the sugar (use a little more or less if you like). Stir to dissolve.

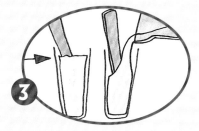

Pour the mixture into ice-block moulds (leaving a little space).

Leave overnight in a cold part of the freezer. (Don't let them fall over.)

Unmould carefully. Wrap in plastic, seal, and keep frozen hard.

Make more, so you have plenty for your friends on hot days!

Chocolate Pudding

Here is a treat that everyone who likes chocolate pudding can make after school. If you like, add sliced banana, too.

Get out a little bowl. If you don't have one, use a cup.

Carefully measure the custard powder, sugar and cocoa into the bowl or cup.

Stir with a teaspoon until you can't see any lumps.

Stir in half the milk, mix well, add the rest of the milk and stir again.

Take out the spoon. Microwave on high for 1 minute, then stir again.

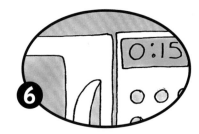

Microwave for 15 seconds or until it rises up around the edge, then stop.

Take out, and stir until the pudding looks thick, brown and smooth.

Put back in the microwave for 10 more seconds if it is not thick enough.

Lie cling film on pudding to prevent skin. When cool, add banana slices.

Banana & Chocolate Chip Muffins

These muffins are kids' favourites! Made as mini-muffins, they freeze well and will thaw in school lunch boxes.

Find everything you need before you start cooking

2 cups self-raising flour
1/2 cup sugar
1/2 cup chocolate chips
1/2 tsp salt

100g butter
1 large egg
1 cup milk
1 tsp vanilla essence
1 cup (2–3) very ripe bananas, mashed

1. Put the oven rack just below middle. Turn the oven on to heat at 220°C.

2. Spray 24 mini-muffin (or 12 larger) muffin pans with non-stick spray.

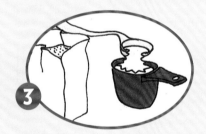

3. Stir the flour, then spoon it into the cup. Don't shake or bang the cup.

4. Measure flour, sugar, chocolate chips & salt into a bowl. Mix with a fork.

5. Melt the butter in another container. Add egg, milk, and vanilla and mix.

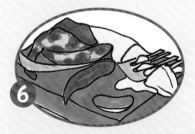

6. Mash the ripe bananas, add to the liquids and mix well with the fork.

Tip the liquids into the flour mixture, all at once.

Stir together until the flour is wet, but mixture still looks lumpy.

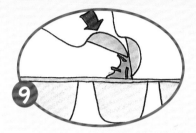

Use two spoons to drop mixture into muffin tins. Don't stir it any more.

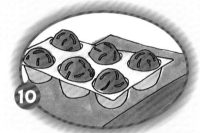

Bake for 10–15 minutes until golden brown, and until centre feels firm.

After 2 minutes lift muffins out on to a rack to cool. Freeze when cold.

Pikelets

Pikelets can be made fast, since they don't have to be cooked in an oven. They are nice plain, but they are good for special occasions, too.

HOT!

Heat a frypan. (Use a high heat setting if frypan is electric.)

Dip an ordinary tablespoon in hot water. Measure the syrup with it.

Put in bowl with butter. Warm to soften both. Mix in sugar, milk and egg.

Sprinkle the flour on top, then mix with a beater just until smooth.

HOT!

Rub surface of the hot frypan with a little butter on a paper towel.

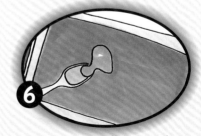

Drop some mixture off the tip of a tablespoon to make a round pikelet.

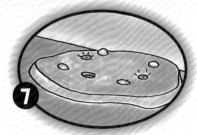

When a bubble bursts on top of the pikelet, it is time to turn it over.

It is cooked when the centre springs back when you touch it.

If pikelet is thick and does not spread, add extra milk to mixture.

Cook all the batter. Turn up the heat if the pikelets are not brown enough

OR turn heat down if pikelets are too brown when the first bubble bursts.

Gingernuts

These are really easy to make because you stir everything together in a pot. It's fun making lots of little gingernuts instead of big ones!

Find everything you need before you start cooking

For 80 small biscuits:

100g butter
1 Tbsp golden syrup
1 cup sugar
1–2 tsp ground ginger
1 tsp vanilla
1 large egg
1 3/4 cups standard flour
1 tsp baking soda

1 Put the oven rack just below middle. Turn the oven on to heat at 180°C.

HOT!

2 Warm the butter in a medium-sized pot and take off the heat when melted.

3 Dip an ordinary tablespoon into hot water, then measure the syrup with it.

4 Add the syrup, sugar, ginger (more for a stronger flavour) and vanilla.

5 Add the egg and mix well with a stirrer or wooden spoon.

6 Sift in the flour and baking soda, then mix everything together again.

7 Stand pot in cold water to cool the biscuit mixture so it is firmer.

8 With wet hands, roll teaspoonsful of biscuit mixture into small balls.

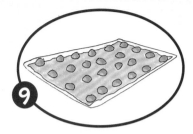

9 Put balls on baking trays lined with baking paper, leaving room to spread.

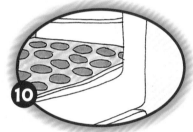

10 Bake 1 tray at a time, for about 10 minutes, until golden brown.

11 Lift onto racks to cool, then store in airtight jars.

Chocolate Chip Cookies

Pack these in lunches or enjoy them after school with a glass of cold milk and an apple or banana. It's hard to think of anything nicer!

Find everything you need before you start cooking

75g butter
1/2 cup brown sugar
1/2 cup white sugar
1 large egg
1/2 cup chocolate chips
1/2 tsp baking soda
1 cup standard flour

Put oven rack just below the middle. Turn the oven on to heat at 180°C.

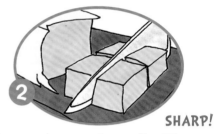

SHARP!

Using marks on pack, cut off a 75g slice of butter. Cut slice in four.

Microwave in bowl for 1 minute or melt in pot until just liquid.

Firmly press brown sugar into measuring cup.

Stir both sugars and egg into the butter and beat well with a fork.

Sprinkle the chocolate chips into the bowl. (Don't eat them!)

Sift in the baking soda and flour, then mix everything together well.

Cover an oven tray with baking paper so the biscuits won't stick.

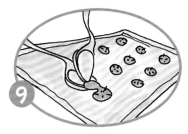

Using 2 spoons, put half mixture in 12 piles. Leave room for spreading.

HOT!

Bake for 8–10 minutes, or until golden brown, then cook the rest.

While warm, lift onto rack. When cold, put in airtight jars.

Orange Slice

With a lovely orange flavour, this is as popular in lunch boxes as it is for dessert. Keep it in the freezer so it is there whenever you want it.

Find everything you need before you start cooking

100g butter
1/2 of a 400g can sweetened condensed milk
finely grated rind of 1 orange
1 cup fine desiccated coconut
1 packet (250g) wine biscuits

For the icing:
25g (2 Tbsp) butter
1 cup icing sugar
about 1 Tbsp orange juice

about 23 cm square, shallow tin

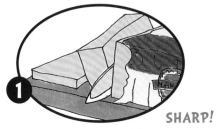

SHARP!

Cut off the butter you need for the slice, and also for the icing.

HOT!

Warm the butter for the slice in a medium sized pot until melted.

Take butter off heat, pour in the condensed milk and stir together.

Finely grate all the orange rind from an orange. Stir it and coconut in.

Break the biscuits. Put the pieces in a big plastic bag. Close bag loosely.

Bang the bag with a rolling pin until all the biscuits are in small crumbs.

Mix the crumbs into the pot. Press mixture into the buttered tin.

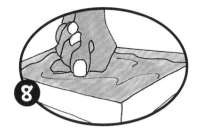

Mixture need not fill the whole tin. Push down well and level the top.

For icing, put soft butter in a clean bowl. Add the icing sugar and juice.

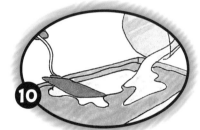

Mix icing with a table knife, then spread smoothly over the base.

Make wiggles on top, chill until firm, then cut into fingers or squares.

Butterscotch Fingers

This three layered shortcake has a yummy butterscotch layer in the middle. It tastes good any time, and keeps well in the freezer for weeks.

Find everything you need before you start cooking

125g butter
1/2 cup sugar
1 large egg
1 tsp vanilla
1 cup self-raising flour
1 cup standard flour

Filling:
100g butter
2 rounded Tbsp golden syrup
400g can sweetened condensed milk

Put the oven rack below the middle. Turn the oven on to 180°C.

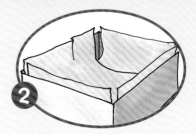

Line a 23x23 or 23x33cm baking tin with 2 strips of baking paper.

Cut the butter in 9 pieces. Warm in a large pot until it starts to melt.

Take off heat and beat in the sugar, egg and vanilla with a stirrer.

Stir in flours until crumbly, then squeeze into a ball, using your hands.

Break 3/4 of the dough into bits, put in baking tin and pat evenly flat.

Make filling. Melt butter. Measure syrup in a hot wet spoon and stir in.

Add the condensed milk, mix well, then pour over unbaked mixture in the tin.

Grate the other 1/4 of the dough on top, using a grater with large holes.

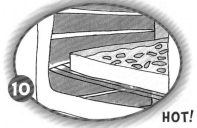

HOT!

Bake for 30–45 minutes until crust is golden and filling has browned.

SHARP!

Leave 2 hours. Cut into fingers with a sharp knife dipped in hot water.

Elizabeth's Carrot Cake

Find everything you need before you start cooking

For the cake:
2 large eggs
1 cup brown sugar
3/4 cup Canola (or other) oil
1 tsp vanilla
1 tsp grated lemon or
   orange rind
2 cups finely grated carrot
1 1/4 cups standard flour
2 tsp cinnamon
2 tsp mixed spice
1 tsp baking soda
1 tsp salt

For the icing:
1 Tbsp butter, warmed
1/2 tsp finely grated lemon
   rind
1 1/2 Tbsp lemon juice
about 1 1/2 cups icing sugar

20 cm square cake tin

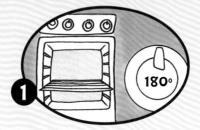

1 Put oven rack just below middle. Turn the oven on to heat at 180°C.

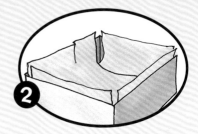

2 Line cake tin with two strips of baking paper.

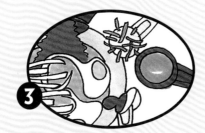

3 Beat eggs, sugar, oil, vanilla and rind together until thick and smooth.

4 Grate carrots, measure by pressing into the cup and stir into the bowl.

5 Sift in the flour, cinnamon, spice, baking soda and salt.

6 Stir gently until smooth, then pour into the lined tin.

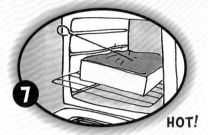

7 **HOT!**

Bake 45 minutes or until centre is firm and a skewer comes out clean.

8 Take carefully out of the tin when cool. Leave on rack to get cold.

9 For icing, warm butter until soft. Add the grated rind and lemon juice.

10 Stir in enough sifted icing sugar to make icing which is not runny.

Everybody seems to love this cake. It is our favourite way to eat carrots! (Use a food processor for grating and mixing if you like.)

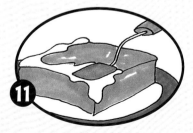

11 Spread carefully over the cake. Cut the cake when icing is cold.

Chocolate Cake

Find everything you need before you start cooking

125g butter
1/2 cup golden syrup
2 large eggs
1 1/2 cups milk
1 cup sugar
2 cups standard flour
1/4 cup cocoa powder
2 tsp baking powder
2 tsp baking soda

Chocolate Icing:
2 Tbsp butter
1 Tbsp cocoa powder
2 Tbsp water
1 1/2 cups icing sugar

whipped cream, if you like

1. Put oven rack below the middle. Turn oven to heat at 180°C. with no fan.

2. Line bottom of a 23cm round cake tin with baking paper and spray sides.

3. Melt the butter in a pot. Measure syrup and mix with the butter.

4. Put eggs, milk and sugar in a large bowl and beat well with an egg beater.

5. Sift the flour, cocoa, baking powder and soda into the bowl. Beat to mix.

6. Add the melted butter and syrup and beat again. Pour into the tin.

7

HOT!

Bake 40 minutes or until a skewer poked into the centre comes out clean.

8

Cool cake on rack. If you like, cut cake in half. Fill with whipped cream.

9

For icing, warm the butter, cocoa and water together until butter melts.

10

Take off heat. Sift in icing sugar. Mix until smooth. Spread on cake.

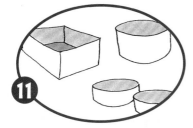

11

If you prefer, bake this cake in a 23x33cm tin or two round tins.

Make this for a weekend treat, to celebrate the birthday of someone special, or just to have fun cooking with a friend.
It tastes good!

Chocolate Truffles

Truffles don't need to be cooked. You make them, then keep them firm and cold in the refrigerator or freezer until you want to eat them.

Find everything you need before you start cooking

125g butter
1/2 of a 250g packet wine biscuits
1/4 cup cocoa powder
1 cup icing sugar
1/2 cup coconut
3 Tbsp orange juice

extra coconut for rolling

If you like:
1/4 chopped walnuts
1/4 chopped sultanas

Cut butter into 9 squares. Warm until soft in large bowl. Do not melt.

If you have a food processor, make the biscuits into crumbs and mix everything in it.

OR Break the biscuits into pieces and put them in a big plastic bag.

Bang the bag with a rolling pin until all the biscuits are crumbs.

Shake through sieve into large bowl. Bang the big pieces of biscuit again.

Sift cocoa and icing sugar into bowl. Add coconut and beat well to mix.

7 Add the orange juice and beat again to mix it in.

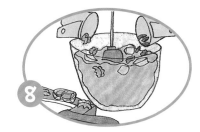

8 Stir in chopped walnuts and sultanas if you want them in the truffles.

9 If the mixture is very soft, cool it in the refrigerator for 10 minutes.

10 With wet hands roll small spoonfuls in balls. Shake in bowl with coconut.

11 Refrigerate for several hours until firm, then pack in airtight jars.

Easy Coconut Ice

This recipe is good for beginners. It always sets, is never too hard, and may be eaten half an hour after it is made! It makes a good gift, too.

Find everything you need before you start cooking

- 1/2 of a 400g can sweetened condensed milk
- 2 cups medium or fine desiccated coconut
- 2 cups icing sugar
- 1 tsp vanilla
- 1 Tbsp raspberry jelly crystals
- Or 1/4 tsp raspberry essence and 4-6 drops red food colouring
- 4×25cm squares of plastic cut from plastic bags

Measure the condensed milk, coconut, icing sugar and vanilla into a bowl.

Mix with a stirrer or fork until evenly mixed and free of lumps.

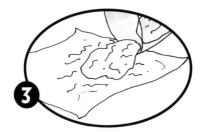

Lift half the mixture onto a piece of plastic sprinkled with extra coconut.

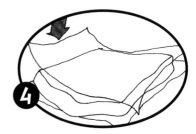

Put another plastic on top of it and pat it out into a 20cm square.

Mix the jelly crystals into the remaining mixture until it looks evenly pink.

OR stir in the raspberry essence and enough red colour to look pale pink.

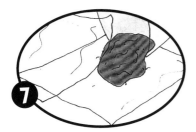

7 Pat mixture into another 20cm square as before, on more plastic.

8 Lift the pink square on to the white square, so their tops are touching.

9 Press together and leave to stand in a cool place for about 30 minutes.

SHARP!

10 Cut into squares with a sharp knife.

11 Eat within 2 days or freeze in a covered box, for up to 3 months.

Fabulous Fudge

Find everything you need before you start cooking

1 cup sugar
1/4 cup cocoa powder, optional*
100g butter
1/4 cup golden syrup
400g can sweetened condensed milk (not low fat)
1 tsp vanilla
1/4 cup chopped walnuts, optional

* Add cocoa for chocolate fudge. Leave it out for caramel fudge.

20cm square tin

TAKE CARE. This mixture gets VERY HOT.

Use a microwave bowl which takes high heat.

CHECK WITH AN ADULT.

1 Butter or non-stick spray the tin. (A loose bottomed tin is good!)

2 Put the sugar (and cocoa) in a dry bowl. Stir until well mixed.

SHARP!

3 Cut the block of butter into 9 cubes and put them on top of the sugar.

4 Add the golden syrup, using a measure which has been dipped in hot water.

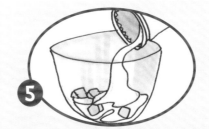

5 Tip the condensed milk evenly over everything else.

HOT!

6 Microwave on High for about 10–12 minutes, stirring every 2 minutes.

It is ready when brown and a little dropped in cold water forms a soft ball.

Move bowl to bench. Leave for 2 minutes. Stir in vanilla (and nuts, if using).

Stir or beat for several minutes, until it is thicker and is not so shiny.

Quickly, before it gets too hard, pour it into the tin. Smooth the surface.

A smooth and creamy treat! You can make it caramel or chocolate flavoured, or add nuts, so you will never get sick of it. Have fun!

SHARP!

Cool, then cut into squares with a sharp knife. Eat, or freeze any extra.

Both of these toffees are good to eat yourself or give to someone special. Always keep toffee in airtight jars to stop it getting sticky.

Find everything you need before you start cooking

1 cup sugar
1/4 cup water
1 Tbsp wine vinegar
25g (2 Tbsp) butter

1 cup roasted peanuts
(for peanut toffee)

1 Put the sugar, water and vinegar in a small pot over low heat.

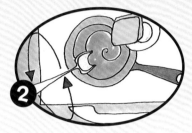

2 Stir just until the sugar dissolves, then add the butter and raise heat.

HOT!

3 Heat so bubbles cover the surface but toffee does not boil over or brown.

4 Every few minutes, drop drops of toffee into a dish of cold water.

5 When a cold drop will break when you bite it, the toffee is cooked enough.

HOT!

6 Raise heat a little until the toffee turns light brown, like a caramel.

HOT!

For plain toffee, drop little rounds onto a buttered oven tray.

For peanut toffee, warm the peanuts in the microwave on High for 45 sec.

HOT!

Tip the warm peanuts into the pot of toffee and stir with a dessert spoon.

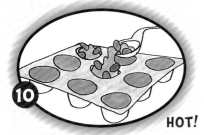

HOT!

Drop teaspoonsful into buttered mini muffin pans or pour on buttered tray.

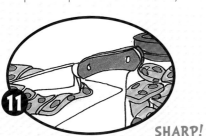

SHARP!

Mark in squares when partly set. Break when hard. Store in airtight jar.

Index

Published by Hyndman Publishing
325 Purchas Road
RD 2, Amberley 7482
ISBN 9781877168208
©TEXT: Alison Holst
©ILLUSTRATIONS: Hyndman Publishing
ILLUSTRATIONS: Seth Kelly
PHOTOGRAPHER:Lindsay Keats
Originally published as Step by Step –
Snacks, Light Meals and Treats.

The recipes in this book have been carefully
tested by the author. The publisher and the
author have made every effort to ensure that
the instructions are accurate and safe, but
they cannot accept liability for any resulting
injury or loss or damage to property
whether direct or consequential.

Because ovens and microwave ovens
vary so much, you should use the cooking
times suggested in recipes as guides only.
The first time you make a recipe, check it
at intervals to make sure it is not cooking
faster, or more slowly than expected.

Always follow the detailed instructions given
by the manufacturers of your appliances
and equipment, rather than the more
general instructions given in these recipes.

For details on the stirrers used in
some of the pictures and other
useful products please visit our
website at www.holst.co.nz